New Dimensions
IN THE
WORLD OF READING

★HERE COMES THE BAND!

PROGRAM AUTHORS

James F. Baumann	Roselmina Indrisano	P. David Pearson
Theodore Clymer	Dale D. Johnson	Taffy E. Raphael
Carl Grant	Connie Juel	Marian Davies Toth
Elfrieda H. Hiebert	Jeanne R. Paratore	Richard L. Venezky

Contributing Author: Rosann Englebretson

COVER ILLUSTRATOR
Spotlight

Jack Davis

▼ Jack Davis drew the funny animal band on the cover of this book. The barnyard animals are about to begin playing their music to a crowd of wild animals.

▼ He liked to run and play with other kids when he was your age. He also loved to draw. So he tells first graders, "Take time every day to do what you feel like doing."

SILVER BURDETT GINN

NEEDHAM, MA   MORRISTOWN, NJ

ATLANTA, GA   DALLAS, TX   DEERFIELD, IL   MENLO PARK, CA

Theme

Animals, ANIMALS

I Had a Cat

I had a cat, and the cat pleased me.
I fed my cat by yonder tree.
Cat goes fiddle-i fee!

5

Have You Seen My Duckling?

Nancy Tafuri

7

Early one morning...

13

14

Have you
seen my
duckling?

16

17

Have you seen my duckling?

18

19

Have
you seen
my duckling?

Have you seen my duckling?

Have you seen my duckling?

24

25

27

Have you seen my cat ?
Eric Carle

Dedicated to all the cats in my life

Have you seen my cat?

Have you seen
my cat?

37

This is not <u>my</u> cat!

38

Have you seen my cat?

39

This is not
<u>my</u> cat!

40

41

This is not <u>my</u> cat!

42

This is not <u>my</u> cat!

Have you seen my cat?

This i

44

46

Have you seen my cat?

47

This is not <u>my</u> cat!

48

Have you seen my cat?

49

This is not my cat!

Have you seen
my cat?

43

This is not <u>my</u> cat!

Have you seen my cat?

45

This is not my cat!

46

Have you seen my cat?

This is not <u>my</u> cat!

48

Where is my cat?

Have you seen my cat?

53

55

Lion

Bobcat

Panther

Tiger

56

Puma

Jaguar

Cheetah

Persian cat

WHAT A DAY!

By Anna Kate Winsey

Illustrated by Lisa Campbell Ernst

What a day!
Cat came to play.

59

What a day!
Dog came to play.

WHAA WAA!

What a day!
Duck came to play.

62

What a day!
Hen came to play.

TOOTLE-E-TOOT!

65

What a day!
Pig came to play.

BOOM!
BOOM!

67

Tweetle-e-Tweet!

What a day!
Skunk came to play.

68

Here comes the band!

70

71

72

Rosie's Walk

By PAT HUTCHINS

Rosie the hen went for a walk

across the yard

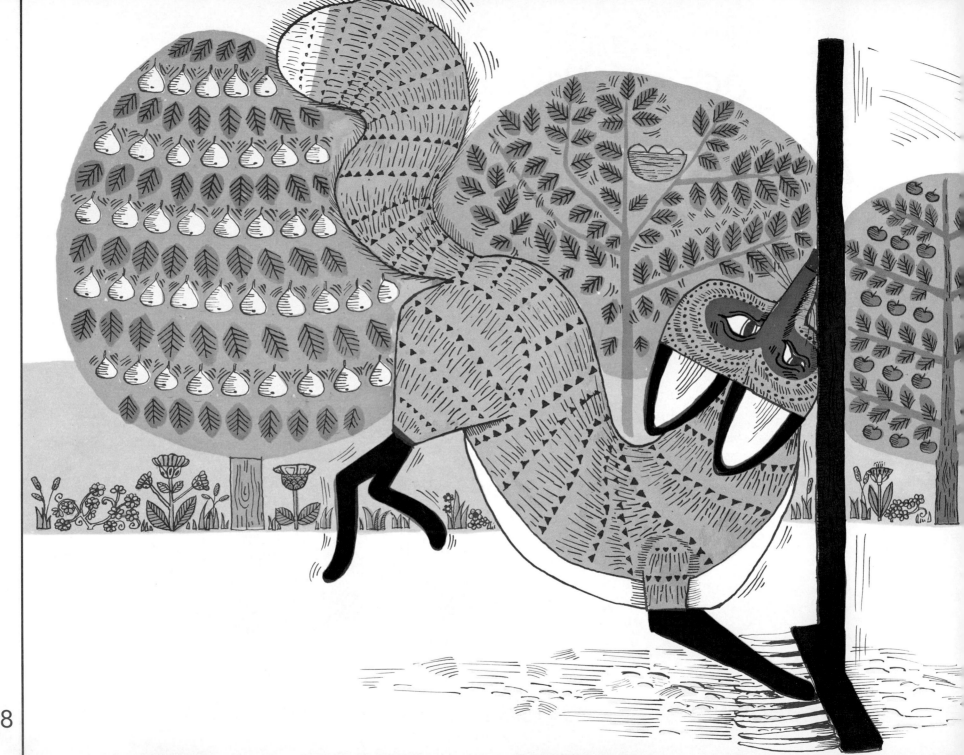

around

the

pond

83

over the haystack

past the mill

88

through the fence

95

under the beehives

and
got back
in time
for dinner.

ABOUT THE
Authors & Illustrators

Eric Carle

When he was in first grade, Eric Carle loved to draw and paint. His teacher knew he was good at drawing. Today, Eric Carle writes and draws pictures for his own children's books. Just like the pictures in the story *Have you seen my cat?* many of his pictures are made of paper.

Pat Hutchins

Pat Hutchins had six brothers and sisters in her family. They lived in the country and watched the animals that lived in the fields and the woods. Now she writes books about the things she saw when she was growing up. *Rosie's Walk* is about a hen in the barnyard. Do you think Pat Hutchins knew a hen like Rosie when she was little?

Nancy Tafuri

Nancy Tafuri wrote the story and drew the pictures for *Have You Seen My Duckling?* She wanted to be an artist when she was very small. Her first job as an artist was drawing pictures for the covers of books. Now she writes the story and draws pictures for the whole book.